Book Description

This book is all about girl power! _~~ut now women advocated for equal rights, education, and healthcare. It focuses on women from around the world, and how they stood up for what they believed in to make their mark on history. Fighting against racism, terrorism, and sexism, these powerful women have changed the world and opened doors that no one else could!

Embark on this journey with me as we take a peek into the lives of 10 women who have changed the world. Great women like Florence Nightingale, Michelle Obama, and Malala Yousafzai, among others, have been honored in this book. Their life stories, their experiences—everything that played a vital part in who they are today— have been explored in the following stories.

Formidable Women Who Changed the World

Learn about the ten most influential women of all time, and the legacy they had upon the world

Paragon Publishing

from various sources. Please consult a licensed professional before attempting any techniques outlined in this book.

By reading this document, the reader agrees that under no circumstances is the author responsible for any losses, direct or indirect, that are incurred as a result of the use of the information contained within this document, including, but not limited to, errors, omissions, or inaccuracies.

Table of Contents

Introduction

Throughout history, there have been many world-changing events: Records were broken, dreams were achieved, and doors were opened for the future by both men and women. Whenever we think of significant world changers, names like Barack Obama, Martin Luther King, and Nelson Mandela tend to quickly pop into our minds. But there are also many women who have ignited such major changes in the world; there are women who have dared to demand their place in society and fight for what is right.

The sacrifices that they have made and the pain that they have suffered through have motivated them to push forward and never give up on their goals. What these 10 women have achieved, no man has ever achieved. The commitment, courage, determination, and passion that these women have displayed amidst their struggle is truly remarkable. Get ready to be educated, motivated, and inspired to make a difference in the world, and remember that every change, no matter how small, can make an extraordinary difference.

Chapter 1: The Lady with the Lamp: Florence Nightingale

Who was Florence Nightingale?

Better known as "the lady with the lamp," Florence Nightingale was a woman with an immense passion for nursing and caring for the sick and wounded. She was born in Florence, Italy on May 12, 1820, which is where she got her name. As a young woman, she was often described as being beautiful, slender, and graceful and always seen adorning a bright, endearing smile. In February 1837, her first experiences began with God, and over the years, she would go on to have many more similar experiences which she interpreted as being calls from God.

Florence ultimately knew that nursing was the only thing she was meant to do in life. Her strong and steadfast desire to help and serve others would become the primary driving force behind her willingness to study nursing. She faced rejection and anger from her mother and her sisters due to her choosing her passion over marriage. However, she knew what she wanted, and she stayed true to herself and pursued her dreams. Florence didn't let people's opinions of her hold her back from doing what she was called to do. While disobeying her parents must have led to her experiencing her own pain and feelings of abandonment, Florence did not give up and because she was so steadfast in her decisions, she has become an inspiring woman who is beloved by millions of people around the world.

Family background

Born into a wealthy family and part of an elite British society, Florence could not bring herself to enjoy or take part in many affluent social gatherings, and she avoided the spotlight as much as she could. She was the youngest of two daughters. Her mother, Frances Nightingale, came from a merchant background and loved socializing with people of a higher social standing. Her father, William Edward Nightingale, was a wealthy landlord who owned many properties from Lea Hurst to Hampshire. The family moved back to England in 1821.

Florence was educated in Mathematics, German, Italian, and French. From a young age, she loved tending to the poor and sick people in the village, and as time went on, realised that being a nurse was her calling in life. Her parents did not approve of her becoming a nurse and they forbade her from pursuing her calling. They believed that being a nurse was a low and demeaning job, and instead, wanted her as a

Nightingale to marry a rich man ensuring that her social standing remained intact. However, getting married was something that Florence could not see herself doing. As a result, in 1850, Florence Nightingale enrolled in nursing school at the Institution of Protestant Deaconesses in Germany.

How Florence contributed to the Crimean War

The Crimean War broke out in October of 1853, and Florence's contribution during this war became the stuff of legends. When she received news about the horrific conditions of the wounded soldiers at the military hospital at Scutari, Nightingale became very disturbed and upset, and decided to go to Scutari. On October 21 in 1854, Florence Nightingale and a staff of 38 volunteer nurses were sent to the Ottoman Empire. She arrived in Scutari in early November 1854 and found the conditions at the hospital to be dreadful. The manner in which the wounded soldiers were treated was unacceptable to Florence.

There was a shortage of medication, the nursing staff was overworked, the sanitary conditions were sickening, and many infections and diseases were spreading all over the hospital. The patients could not be fed properly because there was a shortage of food; the equipment necessary for food production was not functioning and because of this, food could not be prepared. Nightingale was extremely troubled after seeing the horrible things that had been occurring at this hospital. She knew that she had to intervene and make a change.

Approximately 4,000 soldiers died during Florence's first winter at Scutari. More soldiers passed away from illnesses such as typhoid fever, cholera, dysentery, and typhus, than from the wounds which they had suffered during battle. The hospital was overcrowded and there wasn't enough ventilation, the toilets and sanitary conditions were gruesome, and there was little means and opportunity to practice good hygiene. However, within six months of Florence working at the hospital, the sanitary commission had been sent out to Scutari by the British government.

The change that was ignited by Florence Nightingale

Two of the main things that were taken care of by the sanitary commission, was that the sewers had been flushed out and the ventilation was improved. This simple yet important change greatly impacted the overall hygiene of the hospital. Florence also sent in a plea to the British government to help find a solution for the poor facilities in the hospital, and so the British government commissioned Isambard Kingdom Brunel to design a hospital that could be built in England and shipped to the Dardanelles.

Renkioi Hospital was the result of Florence's efforts and it was managed by Edmund Alexander Parkes. Renkioi Hospital had a death rate that was one-tenth less than the death rate at Scutari. By implementing good hygiene practices among the patients and the staff, and by calling for the sanitary commission to come and take care of the issues surrounding the sewage and ventilation, Florence drastically reduced the death rate from 42% to 2%. A humble woman, Florence never claimed credit for the life-saving changes she implemented in the war hospital.

Despite the soldiers' injuries, Florence knew in her heart that they did not die from their wounds. She believed that these soldiers passed away due to the terrible conditions at the hospital: Poor nutrition, lack of clean bedding and supplies, and the overworking of the staff and the soldiers. When Florence returned to Britain, she began investigating and collecting evidence on the health of the army and she brought her findings to the Royal Commission. Evidence showed that most of the people were killed due to the unsanitary living conditions of the hospital.

'The Lady with the Lamp"

Florence Nightingale gained the nickname 'The Lady with the Lamp" during the Crimean War. A report in *The Times* newspaper stated that "Nightingale was a ministering angel, without any exaggeration in these hospitals, and as her slender form glides quietly along each corridor, every poor fellow's face softens with gratitude at the sight of her. When all the medical officers have retired for the night and silence and darkness has settled down among these miles of prostate sick, she may be observed alone, with a little lamp in her hand, making her solitary rounds" (Cooke, 1913).

Florence Nightingale's career in later life

During a public meeting in the Crimea on November 29, 1855, The Nightingale Fund was established for the training of nurses. This was a way of showing gratitude while recognizing the work of Florence during the war. The fund received an outpouring of generous donations and Nightingale received 45,000 euros from the fund to open the Nightingale Training School at St. Thomas hospital. She proceeded to open the training school on July 9 in 1860 and the first set of trained nightingale nurses began to work at the Liverpool Workhouse Infirmary on the 16th of May in 1865. Today, the school is called the Florence Nightingale School of Nursing and Midwifery. America's first trained nurse, Linda Richards, was mentored by Florence, and she was able to return to the United States as a fully trained nurse. Richards had adequate knowledge and training in nursing, so she began establishing professional nursing schools in the U.S.

In closing

Florence had a major impact in the way nurses worked and treated their patients. Her training in various areas of nursing such as sanitation and patient care were instrumental in laying the foundation for trained, professional nursing today. The change she inspired in the world was remarkable and courageous. Florence died at the age of 90 in August of 1910. Her memorial monument stands proud in the cloister of the Basilica of Santa Croce in Florence, Italy.

Chapter 2: The Dedicated Political Activist: Emmeline Pankhurst

Who was Emmeline Pankhurst?

Emmeline Pankhurst was a political activist who fought for women's right to vote. She is known for organizing the UK suffragette movement. She was named one of the 100 most important people of the 20th century by *The Times* newspaper in 1999.

Emmeline Pankhurst's background and early life

Emmeline Goulden was born on the 15th of July, 1858, in Manchester, England. She always believed that her actual birthday was on the 14th of July though, Bastille Day, as she felt a connection with the female revolutionaries who had stormed the Bastille in France on that fateful day.

Family background

Born into a family of politicians, Emmeline's mother was Sophia, a Manx woman from the Isle of Man. The Isle of Man was the first country to grant women the right to vote in 1881. Her father was Robert Goulden, a manufacturer who came from a humble family in Manchester, who had their own backgrounds in politics. Emmeline had four other sisters. She was the oldest among them. Shortly after she was born, their family moved to Seedley where her father became involved in local politics. He also owned a theatre in Salford, and he played the lead in many plays.

Emmeline derived a love and appreciation for theatrics and drama from her father, which she later used to her benefit in social activism. She became involved in politics, along with her siblings, from a young age, a practice encouraged by her parents. This is where Emmeline's political interest began and she learned many things from her parents. One thing that was certain about Emmeline was that she enjoyed reading books. From the tender age of three, she started reading books, and by the time she was nine, she had read and enjoyed books written by John Bunyan. One of Emmeline's favorite books was a three-volume treatise, written by Thomas Carlyle about the French Revolution.

Those books had an amazing impact on her and became her inspiration to fight for what is right and just. Although Emmeline loved reading, she was not able to attend school and become educated like her brothers. Her parents believed that girls should stay at home and learn to be an ideal homemaker; they had to learn how to cook well and take care of a home so that they would become good wives to their husbands, whilst her brothers went off to school to become educated.

What inspired Emmeline?

Emmeline's parents had political backgrounds and they became involved in women's suffrage. She would notice her mother reading *The Women's Suffrage Journal* on a regular basis, which was edited by Lydia Becker. Emmeline admired Lydia and grew fond of her work. One afternoon, when Emmeline was around 14 years old, she insisted on attending a meeting with her mother where Lydia Becker was speaking. Emmeline was completely captivated by what Lydia spoke about and she left that meeting as a deep-rooted suffragist.

Emmeline and Richard find love

At the young age of 20, Emmeline struck up a romance with Richard Pankhurst, who was aged 44. As it happened, he was a barrister for women's suffrage and he fought for their rights to have the freedom to vote, freedom of speech, and the right to be educated. He wanted to remain a bachelor so that he could serve the public 100%. As their relationship grew, Emmeline offered Richard the idea of entering into a free union instead of getting married, however, Richard refused on the basis that Emmeline would not be accepted into politics if she was unmarried. As such, they tied the knot at St. Luke's Church in Pendleton on the 18th of December, 1879.

Women's Franchise League; a stepping stone

In 1888, Emmeline joined the Parliament Street Society group (PSS), which was created by Lydia Becker to take a stand on suffrage and to advocate for single and married women to vote. However, there were a few members of the PSS who were reluctant to advocate on behalf of married women because they believed that these women's husbands could vote for them. This did not sit right with Emmeline and so she decided to leave the PSS.

Emmeline and her husband had formed their own group which was dedicated to voting rights for all women, both single and married. The Women's Franchise League (WFL) was inaugurated on the 25th of July in 1889. The first members of the WFL were Josephine Butler, Elizabeth Wolstenholme Elmy, and Harriet Eaton Stanton Blatch. The WFL was an organisation that didn't only advocate for women's rights to vote, but also for their equal rights in the event of a divorce, and for matters regarding inheritance. As radical and as shifting as the group was, they would eventually go their separate ways after two members, Blatch and Elmy, resigned from the group.

The death of Emmeline's husband

Richard had begun to suffer from severe stomach pains and his health was deteriorating fast; he had developed a gastric ulcer. Emmeline and Richard decided to move to Mobberly, with the hopes that a change of environment and some fresh air would help to improve Richard's condition. It did help, and for a while, he started to feel better with such an improvement in his condition that the family moved back to Manchester. Through it all, Emmeline stayed by Richard's side, but on July 5, 1897, whilst on a train from London to Manchester, Emmeline learnt that Richard had passed away through the very newspaper she was reading.

The loss of her husband greatly affected her, and she soon found herself left with a significant amount of debt. She had to move the family to a smaller house and she worked as a Registrar of Births and Deaths in Chorlton. Working in that position, Emmeline gained more insight into how women were treated in her region. Women used to share their stories and life experiences with Emmeline, stories about their sufferings and how men were allowed to be illegitimate whilst their wives had to stay quiet and accept the injustice. By this point, Emmeline could not sit back any longer and merely bear witness to the sorrow and hardships of these women. She decided to take a stand and continue her fight for women's rights.

As hectic as her life was with being a single mother, and working and running a store for extra income, Emmeline still managed to advocate for women's suffrage and for their equal rights. She never let her responsibilities get the best of her, she continued to push forward and carried on her fight. Through her grieving for her husband, and her many failed attempts to get justice for women, Emmeline stayed focused and committed to her passions.

How the WSPU was formed

After the death of her husband, Emmeline went on to create a new woman-orientated group known as The Women's Social and Political Union in 1903. The slogan of the group was "deeds and not words." As time went on, Emmeline encouraged members of the WSPU to stand firm whenever a bill on women's suffrage had the potential to move forward, however, they were greatly disappointed when the bill failed to advance. In the year 1913, the group resorted to militant actions by vandalizing public art, breaking windows and even starting fires. The suffragettes were arrested throughout these many protests and things seemed to get worse.

However, with the arrival of World War One, everything changed. The government released all suffragette prisoners and Emmeline encouraged these women to fill the jobs of men in the factories so that they could go to battle. The contributions made by the women were recognised by the British Government in 1918, and women were finally granted the right to vote. However, women had to be over the age of 30 while the men's age requirement was 21. This was instigated so that women voters never outnumbered male voters.

In closing

In 1928, Parliament gave women equal rights as men to vote, although Emmeline was not alive to witness this momentous occasion. She died mere weeks before, on the 14th of June. Her unwavering devotion and willingness to fight for women's rights was astonishing and awe-inspiring. Emmeline Pankhurst empowered women, not only in England, but around the world. Her commitment and dedication will forever be admired.

Chapter 3: The Brilliant Scientist: Marie Curie

Who was Marie Curie?

Marie Curie is famous for her discovery of radium and polonium, and for her breakthrough treatments for cancer. She was a two-time Nobel Prize winner, the first woman to win a Nobel Prize, and the only person to win a Nobel Prize for findings in two scientific fields.

Marie's background

Born on the 7th of November in 1867, Maria Skłodowska was the youngest of five children born to teachers Boguska and Wladyslaw Skłodowska. Marie came from a poor family as her parents had lost their fortunes and their property because of their involvement in the national Polish uprising. This uprising was aimed at restoring the independence of Poland. This impacted the family deeply, and Marie and her siblings experienced great struggle as a result.

Marie's father was eventually fired from his post, and the only way he could bring an income into the family was through lodging boys in his home. Marie's mother had passed away of tuberculosis when Marie was 10 years old. Three years later, Marie's older sister passed away from typhus, which she contracted from one of the boarders who stayed in their home. An atheist, Marie's father didn't believe in God while her mother had been a devout Catholic. When her mother and sister died, Marie gave up on religion, becoming agnostic as she just didn't know what to believe anymore.

As a young girl, Marie attended a boarding school for girls, and thereafter she attended a gymnasium for girls. She graduated with a gold medal on June 12, 1883. On one occasion, Marie collapsed suddenly, making everyone think that she was depressed. She decided to spend a year with relatives in the countryside, and another year in Warsaw with her father. As a woman, Marie could not enroll in a regular institution for higher education. Instead, Marie and her sister became involved with a floating university, a Polish institute of higher education that accepted women learners.

Her life in Paris and how it influenced her

Marie decided to leave Poland and head for France in 1891. She lived with her sister and brother-in-law for a while before she found a garret that she rented closer to the university. Marie pursued her studies in physics, mathematics, and chemistry at the University of Paris. She was a dedicated student who was so engrossed in her studies that she often forgot to eat. During the cold winters, Marie would use all the clothes she had to stay warm because she did not have enough blankets. She would study during the day and offer tutoring in the evenings just to get by.

Marie received her degree in Physics during the year of 1893. She began working at the industrial laboratory of Gabriel Lippmann, and she continued to study at the University of Paris where she obtained her second degree in 1894. Marie kick-started her career with research and through the investigation of the magnetic properties of different types of steel. Engrossed in her work, Marie wasn't really looking to date anyone. That's when she met Pierre Curie. They both had a passion for science, and that is what drew them to each other. Eventually the two fell in love and Pierre proposed to Marie, but she declined at first because she wanted to go back to her native country of Poland. Pierre convinced Marie that he was ready to move back to her hometown with her in Poland.

During the summer break in 1894, Marie visited her family in Warsaw. She had the notion that she could work in Poland, in her chosen field, but she was denied a position at Krakow University due to sexism. Marie then returned to Paris where she pursued her Ph.D. Pierre and Marie were married on the 26th of July in 1895. Marie had found her soulmate, the one in whom she could depend and share her passion for science. Pierre became her biggest supporter and continued to encourage her to be the best she could be in her field.

Marie's remarkable findings of new elements

Marie and her husband Pierre published a paper together in July 1898, announcing the existence of a new element called "polonium," which they named after Marie's home country of Poland. In December of 1898, they announced the existence of another element named "radium." Marie and Pierre also coined the word "radioactivity."

The Curie's published many scientific papers, around 32 papers, to be exact. There was one particular paper that announced that tumor-forming cells in the human body were destroyed faster when exposed to radium. This was a breakthrough discovery made by Marie and Pierre, and today, it is used to treat cancer in people. Although they discovered this element, the Curies did not patent their discovery, and so another business was developed based on radium.

Nobel Prizes and death of Pierre

Because of Marie and Pierre's great work and research on radiation, they were awarded the Nobel Prize in

Physics. This made Marie the first woman to win a Nobel Prize, which was an extraordinary achievement. The cash prize which they received was used to hire a new lab assistant. The University of Paris had given Pierre both the honor of a professorship, and elected him the Chair of the Physics Department, but they still did not have a proper laboratory to work in. Pierre brought this to the attention of the University, and they agreed to set up a new laboratory for the Curies. However, this lab was not ready until 1906.

On the 19th of April in 1906, tragedy struck and Pierre was killed in an accident. Whilst walking home in rainy weather, he was run over by a horse-driven carriage. He fractured his skull, leading to his death. Marie was devastated by her husband's death. She had lost her life partner and her biggest supporter. In 1906, the University offered Marie the Chair position that had been created for her last husband. Though hesitant, Marie decided to accept the offer. She hoped to establish a world-class laboratory in the memory of her late husband, Pierre Curie. Marie was the first woman to become a professor at the University of Paris.

The University of Paris and the Pasteur Institute joined together to create a radioactive laboratory for Marie, which she headed in 1909. It was called the Radium Institute, now known as the Curie Institute. In 1910, Marie successfully isolated radium. She was awarded a second Nobel Prize in Chemistry in 1911.

World War One and Marie's invention

Marie really outdid her own previous successes during World War One. She believed that the soldiers who were wounded would receive a better prognosis if they were operated upon as soon as possible. Avoiding amputations and actually saving their limbs was possible with Marie's X-ray equipment which she procured. Marie became the director of the Red Cross Radiology Service and she set up the first radiology center in France. It was said that there were over a million soldiers who were X-rayed and treated. She used her remaining Nobel Prize money to buy war bonds that could be used by the state for its soldiers. Marie changed the lives of these soldiers, who could have lost their limbs unnecessarily. Her exceptional developments of the X-ray saved these soldiers' limbs and changed the future of the medical world.

In closing

Marie died on the 4th of July in 1934 at the age of 66. Her cause of death was aplastic anemia, which was said to be caused by her long-term exposure to radiation which had damaged her bone marrow. She achieved so much in her short life and her work has pioneered the future for radiation. Marie Curie changed the world with her education, expertise, and her passion. She will forever be remembered and admired as a female scientist.

Chapter 4: The Record-Breaking Pilot: Amelia Earhart

Who was Amelia Earhart?

Amelia Earhart was the first female aviator who flew across the Atlantic Ocean by herself. She was a best-selling author who wrote about her experiences of flying as a pilot. She also played a huge part in forming The Ninety Nines, which was an organization for female pilots.

Amelia Earhart's background and achievements

Amelia was born on the 24th of July, 1897 in Atchison, Kansas. She was part German and she enjoyed exploring the outdoors with her sister, Grace Muriel Earhart. They both had nicknames for each other: Amelia answered to the name "Meeley" and Grace answered to the name "Pidge." These names followed them into adulthood. The two sisters loved hunting rats with their rifles, climbing trees, and sliding down hills in their sled. Their adventurous spirit and their love for the outdoors turned them into tomboys who were carefree and fearless, and they collected various insects and toads on their outings together.

Family background

Her father, Edwin Erhart, worked as a claims officer for the Rock Island Railroad. However, he was an alcoholic and was forced to retire from his job. Though he desperately tried to beat his addiction and rehabilitate himself, he had no success. Amelia Otis, Amelia's grandmother—whom she was named after—died suddenly. She left behind an inheritance for her daughter which was placed in a trust. Their house was auctioned off along with all of its contents. This event greatly impacted Amelia and she described it as the end of her childhood. Amelia and her sister lived with their grandmother, before her passing, whilst her parents moved. Amelia was fond of her grandmother, so her death caused Amelia much grief.

Amy Earhart eventually took her children to Chicago. Amelia graduated from Hyde Park High School in 1916, though she had a terrible high school experience. Despite her troubled childhood, Amelia would continue to aspire for a future career. She pictured herself as a woman who could work in any male-dominated field. She would often reminisce about the first time she saw an airplane at the Iowa state fair when she was just ten years old. Though she didn't particularly find the airplane interesting, she was fascinated with the idea of flying.

During World War One, Amelia began working as a volunteer nurse after receiving training as a nurse's aide from the Red Cross. She prepared food for the patients who had a special diet to follow and she handed out medication at the dispensary.

The world-changing Spanish flu of 1918

Amelia worked hard as a nurse. She often worked night shifts at the Spadina Military Hospital, and when the Spanish flu hit in 1918, Amelia became sick with pneumonia and maxillary sinusitis. She suffered from pressure and pain around one of her eyes and had mucus drained out from her nostrils and her throat. She was hospitalised because of her pneumonia in November 1918, and later discharged in December 1918.

During these times, there were no antibiotics and Amelia had to undergo many different surgeries to drain out the maxillary sinus. Despite the many attempts, the procedures were not successful and Amelia would experience terrible headaches. She spent a year recovering from her illness, and she spent it at her sister's home. She would read books on poetry and study mechanics to pass her time, but she really could not do much whilst she was recovering.

Amelia meets George

Amelia met publisher George P. Putnum in 1928. They spent a considerable amount of time together before Putnum proposed marriage to Amelia, though it took six times before she finally accepted. They tied the knot on the 7th of February, 1931 in Putnam's parents' house in Connecticut. Amelia often looked at her marriage as a kind of partnership with dual control. She believed that there should be equality in a marriage and neither person should be bound to the other. She wanted to have the freedom to make her own decisions.

Amelia's early flying experiences

When Amelia's parents reunited in 1920, she moved out to Long Beach in California to be with them. Her father took her to visit an airfield where the famous air racer, Frank Hawks, gave Amelia a ride of her life. It was then and there that Amelia finally realised what she wanted to do. She wanted to fly! Amelia had been working a few different jobs: She worked as a photographer, as a truck driver, and as a stenographer for a telephone company. She wanted to take flying lessons, so she managed to save up $1000 for the lessons. She finally had her first lesson on the 3rd of January 1921, a month after her visit to the airfield.

Anita Snook was Amelia's instructor and she conducted the lessons in a Curtiss JN-4 "Canuck." Amelia had to accept the tough conditions that came with aviation training. It required hard work and commitment, and Amelia was more than ready to face any challenge that was thrown at her. She donned a brown leather jacket and cut her hair short, similar to the other women who were training to become pilots. Then, on the 22nd of October in 1922, something extraordinary happened. Amelia set a world record for other female pilots by flying the Airster to an altitude of 14,000 feet. Amelia Earhart received her pilot's licence on May 15, 1923; she was the 16th woman in the U.S. to receive a pilot's licence.

Amelia's unforgettable transatlantic flight experience

One afternoon while Amelia was at work, she received a call from Captain Hilton H. Riley. He called Amelia with a preposition; he wanted to know if she would be interested in flying across the Atlantic Ocean. Charles Lindbergh was the first person to fly solo across the Atlantic Ocean in 1927. Amy Guest was interested in being the first woman to fly solo across the Atlantic Ocean, but she realised that the trip would be too tiring for her to undertake. So, she decided to sponsor the project and find another girl who had the right image to fly across the Atlantic.

Amelia was asked to accompany the pilot Wilmer Stultz and co-pilot Louis Gordon on the flight as a passenger and flight log bookkeeper. The team departed from Trepassey Harbour on 17 June 1928, in a Fokker F.Viib named "Friendship." They landed near Burry Port in South Wales 20 hours and 40 minutes later. Amelia did not pilot the aircraft, mainly because she was not trained for this type of flying. But she knew that one day she would fly across the Atlantic solo.

Amelia and promoting aviation

Amelia accepted a position as an associate editor at *Cosmopolitan Magazine.* She saw an opportunity to promote public acceptance for aviation and to encourage other women to enter into this field. In 1929, Amelia was one of the first aviators who promoted commercial air travel by developing a passenger airline service. Charles Lindbergh was also a part of this momentous occasion, and together they represented Transcontinental Air Transport. They invested their time and their money to set up the first shuttle service which ran between New York and Washington D.C. It was known as the Ludington Airline. She was also the vice president of National Airways.

Amelia's record-breaking, first solo flight across the Atlantic

Although Amelia played a huge role in the transatlantic flight, she still wanted to create a record of her own. She decided that it was time to now pursue her goal of flying solo across the Atlantic Ocean. Shortly after piloting the Avian 7083, Amelia set off on her first solo flight across the Atlantic Ocean. In August 1928, Amelia Earhart became the first woman to fly solo across the Atlantic Ocean and back. Her piloting skills only got better and she became unstoppable.

Her professionalism grew as she was acknowledged by other pilots who flew with her. Amelia began participating in competitive flying races in 1929. She came in fourth place in the "heavy planes" division. Amelia then went on to set a new world altitude record by flying a Pitcairn PCA-2 at an astonishing 18,415 feet. She became involved with the Ninety Nines, an organisation built on promoting and encouraging female pilots in the aviation industry. She was then elected as the organisation's first president in 1930.

In closing

Amelia always advocated for female pilots and encouraged them to pursue their dreams in aviation. She was an ambitious woman who never gave up on her dreams. She opened the doors to the world of aviation for thousands of women from all over the world. Her work in creating a commercial air service bore many fruits over the years. Her achievements are outstanding and unbelievable, but it goes to show that anything is possible, especially if you're a woman.

Chapter 5: A Woman who Fought for Equality: Rosa Parks

Who was Rosa Parks?

Rosa Parks was an African American woman who stood for the civil rights of her people. She was an activist in the civil rights movement and played an important role in the Montgomery bus boycotts.

Rosa Parks and her family

Rosa Louise McCauley, famously known as Rosa Parks, was born on the 4th of February in 1913 in Alabama. Her parents were Leona McCauley, a teacher, and James McCauley, a carpenter. Her great grandmother was a Native American slave and her great grandfather was part Scottish and part Irish. When Rosa's parents separated, she went to live with her mother, her little brother Slyvester, and her grandparents on a farm.

Rosa attended schools that were considered rural, up until she turned 11 years old.

When she was younger, her mother taught her how to sew, and she loved sewing quilts, the first of which she sewed when she was 10 years old. At school, Rosa learned more about sewing and she sewed her first dress, which she wore all the time. Rosa went to a laboratory school which was created by the Alabama State Teachers College for negros. But Rosa had to drop out of college when her mother and her grandmother fell ill. It was now up to Rosa to take care of them and she could no longer make time to study.

Injustice raises its head

Black and white segregation had just started making its way into the communities as the 20th century began. Blacks were not allowed to vote, neither were the underprivileged whites allowed. The laws that were established by Jim Crow were meant to separate whites from blacks everywhere. There was racial segregation at public toilets, at restaurants, at parks, churches and shopping areas, and especially on public transportation such as buses and trains. There was separate seating for whites and blacks on public transport.

Rosa walked to school every day whilst a bus took all the white learners to school. This greatly impacted

Rosa and she began to see the world separated into two: A black world where they were treated unfairly and deprived of living the basic type of life, and a white world, where whites were treated superior to the blacks and life was easier for them. She was often bullied by the white children in her community and she would retaliate by being physical towards them. Rosa became angry and troubled by this and she believed that she would bring an end to it someday.

Rosa's early days of activism

Rosa met a charming barber named Raymond Parks; the two spent a lot of time getting to know each other. They eventually got married in 1932. Raymond was a member of the National Association for the Advancement of Coloured People (NAACP), they were trying to raise money to defend the Scottsboro Boys. These were a group of black men who were wrongly accused of raping two white women. The NAACP believed that they could help these men by providing them with a lawyer who could defend them in court.

Rosa worked multiple jobs during her marriage: She worked as a hospital aid and a domestic worker. Whichever job came her way, she was ready to work. In 1933, Raymond encouraged Rosa to finish her high school diploma. At this time, less than 7% of African Americans had a high school diploma in the U.S. It was important to Raymond that Rosa complete her education. Rosa became active in the civil rights movement in December of 1943. She joined the NAACP's Montgomery chapter and eventually was elected as secretary.

Rosa worked as a secretary until 1957. She worked for Edgar Nixon, the local leader of the NAACP. He believed that women were only productive in the kitchen and nowhere else. Rosa aimed to prove him wrong. In 1944, whilst still holding the position of a secretary, Rosa began investigating the gang rape of Mrs. Recy Taylor, a black woman from Alabama.

Together with the help of other activists, a campaign was organized and named "The Committee for Equal Justice for Recy Taylor." The campaign was described, by *The Chicago Defender*, as the strongest campaign for equal justice to be seen in over a decade. Rosa continued her work in anti-rape activism and helped organize protests for Gertrude Perkins, a black woman who had been raped by two white police officers.

Rosa and her husband Raymond became members of the League of Women Voters in the 1940's. At this time, Rosa also worked as a housekeeper for a white couple named Clifford and Virginia Durr. The couple didn't share the same sentiments for white superiority as many others did. They did not discriminate against her, nor did they believe that they were more superior to the blacks. The couple became good friends with Rosa; they had seen her passion for activism and they encouraged her to attend the Highlander Folk School. This was a center that educated people on activism in worker's rights and in racial equality. They even sponsored Rosa, and she eventually attended the school in the summer of 1955.

Montgomery's harsh laws regarding segregation

Montgomery passed a law in 1900, which segregated all passengers on a bus by their race. The conductors were allowed to assign seats to make sure that everyone complied with the law. White passengers were seated separately from black passengers. According to the law, no passenger would have to move from their seat or stand if the bus was filled to capacity. However, as time passed, the conductors began to bend the rules and require the black passengers to stand or move from their seats when there were no "white's only" seats available.

Whites were assigned to the first four rows of seats on the Montgomery bus, and the rear end of the bus was reserved for the blacks, even though they made up more than 75% of the people who were on the bus. The sections on the bus that were allocated to the different races weren't fixed sections. Rather, they were determined by a movable sign. This allowed the blacks to sit in the middle of the bus, as long as the white seats were not filled up yet. Once the white seats were fully occupied, then the blacks had to move to the back of the bus to allow more white passengers on the bus.

Travelling on the bus became extremely frustrating and infuriating to Rosa. She would often choose to walk rather than to take the bus. There was one horrible experience that Rosa would never forget. One day in 1943, Rosa boarded a Montgomery bus and paid the fare, and moved to a seat. The bus driver, James F. Blake, told Rosa to follow city rules and to get up from her seat and enter the bus again, using the back entrance of the bus instead of the front. Rosa got up and exited the bus, walking towards the back entrance to board the bus again, but as soon as Rosa stepped out of the bus, Blake drove off without her. Rosa vowed never to take his bus again.

"I refuse to move"

On December 1, 1955, Rosa Parks boarded a Montgomery city line bus, at 6 pm in the evening. She paid her fare and sat in the first row of back seats which were reserved for black passengers. Rosa didn't notice that the driver was James F. Blake, the same driver who had ditched her in 1943. Gradually, all of the "whites only" seats filled up. When the bus stopped in front of the Empire Theatre, several white passengers got on. Blake noticed that there were a few white passengers standing, so he proceeded to ask the black passengers to move so that the white passengers would have a seat.

There were a few black passengers who moved and allowed the white passengers to take their seats. But when it was time for Rosa to move, she refused. Thoughts of how blacks were being mistreated passed through her mind, and she was determined to not give in. She stood her ground. When the driver asked her why she wouldn't get up, Rosa said that she didn't see why she had to because she was seated in the right place. The driver then called the police and Rosa was arrested.

The historical Montgomery bus boycott

Edward Nixon spoke to Jo Ann Robinson, a college professor and a member of the Women's Political Council, about the incident involving Rosa Parks. They both decided to take advantage of the opportunity and organised a bus boycott. They handed out over 35,000 handbills which announced the bus boycott. News spread like wildfire among the black churches in the area. They all agreed to continue with the boycott until black drivers were hired and seating was handled on a first-come basis with no discrimination based on color.

Meanwhile, Rosa had been charged with disorderly conduct and violating a local ordinance. She went to trial and was found guilty and charged a fine of $10. The boycott that had been organized by Dixon went on as planned. On that Monday, none of the blacks took the bus. Some went to work by travelling in carpools, others walked more than 20 miles. It didn't matter how hard it made their lives, all they knew was that it had to be done. After the success of the boycott, the group decided that they needed to form another organisation to lead the future boycotts. They formed the organisation called The Montgomery Improvement Association (MIA).

Martin Luther King Jr. was elected president of the organisation. The boycott continued and lasted for 381 days. This took a huge toll on the Montgomery buses' finances. The city finally repealed its laws regarding segregation on buses.

In closing

Rosa Parks had the courage and the determination to make a change in the way the black community was treated. She stood firm for what she believed in and she ignited the flame which spread across the country. She inspired the change the world needed to see and started a movement that brought about a very necessary, very important change.

Chapter 6: A civil rights activist: Coretta Scott King

Who was Coretta Scott King?

Coretta Scott King was a woman who advocated for African American rights and equality. She was a civil rights leader in the 1960's and also the wife of Martin Luther King Jr. She had taken over the struggle on racial inequality and became an active part of the Women's Movement.

Coretta Scott's background

Coretta was born on the 27th of April in 1927, in Heiberger, Alabama. Her parents were Obediah and Bernice Scott, and her grandmother, Delia Scott, was a former slave. Coretta's mother, Bernice, had a beautiful voice and she loved to sing. Coretta's father, Obediah, was one of the first black people to own a car in their town. He was a business owner and ran a clothing shop along with his wife. Coretta's maternal grandparents were Mollie and Martin Van Buran McMurry. They were both half African-American and half Irish descent. Both were born into slavery.

When Coretta was 10 years old, she worked to make some money for her family. Even though the family owned a farm, they weren't wealthy. She had two older sisters who didn't survive their childhood. During the Great Depression, Coretta and her brother Obediah picked cotton to help earn money for the family. Coretta saw herself as a tomboy in her childhood days, as she loved climbing trees and wrestling with boys. Despite her parents being uneducated, they wanted their children to be educated and to go to college when they were older.

Coretta had an opportunity to study music with Walter Anderson; he was the first black person to become the chair of a department at a historically white college. She seized the opportunity and enjoyed learning music. She became active in politics due to her experiences with discrimination at her school. Coretta joined the National Association for the Advancement of Coloured People (NAACP) and the college's committees on race and civil rights. She knew that she wanted to bring about change, no matter how young she was.

Meeting Martin Luther King

Coretta was granted a scholarship to study music in Boston, at the New England Conservatory of Music. It was during her time studying there that she met Martin Luther King Jr., a minister with a promising future. She was a bit hesitant to meet with Martin at first, but finally agreed. Martin was surprised to see how short of stature Coretta was in person, but he told her that she was everything he was looking for in a wife. However, Coretta dismissed him because it was their first date and she was only just getting to know him.

During the first few months of 1952, the couple met up with each other on a regular basis. Martin was pretty sure that he had met the woman who was going to be his wife. He wrote a letter to his mother telling her that he found his wife. His parents visited the couple but had their reservations towards Coretta. They told her that her career in music would be a good choice if she were to marry a Baptist minister. Despite Coretta having a passion for music, she knew that she could not pursue a career in music if she were to marry Martin. But she was drawn to him and she soon knew that he was the one.

Although his parents didn't particularly approve of Coretta, Martin knew that he wanted to marry her and only her. He tried to convince his mother and explained to her that he was going to get his doctorate first, then he would marry Coretta. Once they heard this, Martin's parents agreed to the marriage and gave them their blessings. On the 18th of June 1953, the two got married at Martin's mother's house. The ceremony was performed by Martin's father.

After their marriage, the couple moved to Montgomery, Alabama. Martin accepted an invitation to be the Pastor of Dexter Avenue Baptist Church. This was the same church where the Montgomery Boycott was organized. Coretta and Martin found themselves involved in the Montgomery bus boycott which had been organized upon the arrest of Rosa Parks. Coretta felt like she was involved in something great and that she could finally make a difference in her community.

The Civil Rights Movement and the death of Martin

Martin had become a full-time Pastor at the church by September of 1954. Coretta stayed home and took care of the children while taking part in the church choir and teaching Sunday school. After they became involved in the Montgomery bus boycott, Martin began to receive death threats and nasty phone calls. Coretta would often answer these calls that were threats against her husband. They continued to stand firm in their beliefs, which were based on Biblical teachings. One night, on December 23rd, there was a shooting at their home whilst Martin and Coretta were asleep. Luckily no one was hurt.

Coretta made her first appearance advocating for civil rights legislation on April 25, 1958. She appeared at a concert that was held in the auditorium at Peter High

School. She sang a few songs that were inspired by the Montgomery bus boycott. This was a chance for Coretta to play an active role in the movement and to continue her professional career. When Coretta was visiting Martin's parents in Atlanta, she received news that Martin had been stabbed during one of his book signings. She rushed back home and stayed by his side whilst he recovered in hospital. Once he had recovered, Martin and Coretta went on a four-week tour of India.

Despite surviving that attack, Martin was shot and killed on the 4th of April, 1968 in Memphis, Tennessee. Coretta had a hard time dealing with the death of her husband. She had to find a way to help her children understand that their father was now dead. She was still determined to carry on leading and advocating for civil rights. On the 8th of April, 1968, Coretta and her children decided to carry out a march for sanitation workers, which her husband had planned to do before his death.

Coretta eventually took over the reins of the Civil Rights Movement and she included women's rights, LGBT rights, and world peace. She then founded the King Centre for Nonviolent Social Change in Atlanta, in memory of her late husband. She served as the CEO of the center until she passed the reins to her son, Dexter. This allowed her to focus on her writing and her love for public speaking. She wrote and published her first memoirs in 1969, titled *My Life with Martin Luther King Jr.*

Coretta's fight against apartheid and LGBT

equality

Coretta stood firm in her fight against apartheid and she was a part of many sit-down protests in Washington D.C. She also took a 10-day trip to South Africa, where she met with Allan Boesak and Winnie Mandela. She also met with Mandela, and she described that day as being one of the best days of her life. She made comparisons between the civil rights movement and Mandela's case. She knew that something had to be done so she urged Reagen to approve economic sanctions against South Africa.

She also advocated for world peace. Coretta believed that anything could be achieved without the use of violence; she believed that there was always a better way to get people to listen to you, there was no need to resort to violence to convince people that something is right. The LGBT community was lucky enough to have Coretta fighting for their equality and for their rights. In Washington D.C., in August 1983, she urged that both gay and lesbian people should be included in the civil rights as a protected class.

In closing
Coretta Scott King was a woman who refused to stand in the shadow of her husband, Martin Luther King Jr.; she decided to stand beside him and fight *with,* and after, him. She had her own dreams and aspirations to

bring forth change in racial discrimination and she fought against all types of inequality. Coretta loved her husband, so much so that she made his birthday a national holiday. Her conversations with John F. Kennedy were pivotal in igniting a change for African American voters. Coretta Scott King achieved a lot during her lifetime and her work, and legacy, will never be forgotten.

Chapter 7: World's Best Female Tennis Player: Billie Jean King

Who is Billie Jean King?

Billie Jean King is known as America's former Number 1 tennis player. She is regarded as one of the best female tennis players of all time. Billie Jean King represented the USA at the Federations Cup, where she was the captain, and at the Wightman Cup. Billie Jean is an advocate for gender equality and she has always pioneered social justice.

Billie's family and background

Born as Billie Jean Moffitt on the 22nd of November, 1943 in Long Beach, California, Billie was part of a very conservative Methodist family, and her parents were fairly ordinary. Her mother Betty was a housewife and her father Bill was a firefighter. Both of her parents were very athletic. Betty was a pro at swimming, and Bill ran track and played basketball and baseball. Her brother, Randy Moffitt, became a major league pitcher for the San Francisco Giants, Toronto Blue Jays, and Houston Astros.

Billie loved sports as well, and as a child she played softball and baseball. She joined a softball team of girls who were all older than her by four years. The team did so well together that they eventually went on to win the Long Beach Softball Championship. Her parents suggested that Billie find a sport that was more appropriate however since she was a girl. So, when she was 11 years old, Billie turned to tennis. She bought her very first tennis racket with money she saved and she went for free lessons at the public courts that were conducted by a professional tennis player named Clyde Walker.

Billie was a free-spirited young girl who often did as she pleased. Her first tennis tournaments were hindered because of her belligerent playing styles. At one of the tournaments, Billie wasn't allowed to be a part of the group picture because she didn't have the proper tennis attire, which was a white tennis dress for girls. Instead, she had on shorts that had been sewn by her mom.

Billie knew what she wanted though; she wanted to become the best tennis player in the world, and she said this to her church minister, Bob Richards, a former Olympic champion himself. Billie had set her goal and she was on her way to achieving it. After graduating high school, Billie attended California State University, but dropped out in 1964 because she wanted to focus on tennis.

During her time at Cal State, Bille met Larry King. The couple first met in a library in 1963. They fell madly in love and got engaged whilst Billie was only 20 years old and still in college, and Larry was 19 years old. They got married on September 17, 1965.

How did Billie's career start?

At the age of 15, Billie made her Grand Slam debut at the U.S. championships in 1959. Her coaches were Frank Brenan and Alice Marble, who had won 18 Grand Slam titles during her time as a tennis player. However, she stopped coaching Billie because of her ambition. Billie lost in her first round at the U.S. championships. She started off playing at local, regional, and international tennis championships. Billie was proclaimed as one of the most promising youngsters on the west coast, by *Sports Illustrated*.

At the 1960 Philadelphia and District Grass Court championships, Billie won her first tournament. In her second attempt at the U.S. Championship, Billie lost to Bernice Carr Bukovich in the third round. She also played in the National Girls 18 and under Championships where she lost to Karen Huntse Susman in the final set. As time went on, her tennis rankings went up. Whereas she was ranked number 19 in 1959, by 1960 she was number four. This was the year that kickstarted Billie's career.

In 1961, Harold Guiver raised $2000 to send Billie to Wimbledon. This is when she gained international recognition. Billie partnered with Karen Hantze and they won the women's doubles in their first attempt. Billie was 17 and Karen was 18; this made them the youngest team to win the Wimbledon Doubles title.

Billie Jean King started her career off by being the fifth woman in the history of tennis to win the singles titles at the French Open. She won an amazing 20 career titles at Wimbledon, four in mixed doubles, six in singles and 10 in women's doubles. From 1959 through to 1983, Billie played 51 Grand Slam single's events. She managed to reach the quarterfinals in 40 attempts and the semi-finals 27 times. Billie Jean won 129 singles titles and her prize money totaled $1,966,487.

From 1963 until 1979, Billie was on the winning team seven times at the Federation Cup. Her win-loss career record in the Federations Cup was 52-4 and she won the last 30 matches, which she played before she ended her career. In the Wightman Cup, Billie won her last nine matches and her career win-loss record was 22-4. Out of the 11 years in which Billie participated, the United States won 10 Cups. In her singles matches she won 6-1 against Anne Haydon, 4-0 against Virginia Wade and 1-1 against Christine Truman Janes.

World-changing match

On the 20th of September 1973, a tennis match between Billie Jean King and Bobby Riggs took place. The match was dubbed "the battle of the sexes." Bobby Riggs was named the world's number 1 male tennis player for 1941, 1946, and 1947. He was all too proud of his achievements and expressed that despite being 55 years old, he could still beat any current top female player. He believed that the women's game of tennis was inferior to the men's game.

Billie had previously rejected challenges offered by Riggs, but she accepted a profitable offer of $100,000 in a winner-takes-all match. The match took place in front of 90 million people worldwide with a television audience and 30,492 spectators at the stadium. No match has ever been seen by so many people before or since then. Billie won all three sets, with the first set 6-4, the second set 6-3, and the third set 6-3. This match proved Bobby wrong; women were not inferior to men in tennis. Billie was concerned that if she had lost that match, it would have set the female tennis players back 50 years and it would have affected the tour.

Billie had campaigned for equal prize money for both men and women. She believed that women were not inferior to men in any way and that both genders played a fair game. There were no separate rules for the game for men or women, so why should the prize money be different? In 1973, Billie formed the

Women's Tennis Association and was the first president of the association. Due to her campaigns for equal prize money, the U.S. Championships were the first tournament to offer equal prize money to the participants. She then went on to co-fund the World Team Tennis co-ed and she also started the Women's Sports Foundation, which was dedicated to providing girls and women with access to sports.

In the early 1970's, Billie realised that she was ultimately interested in women sexually. Her personal life took a hit as she began questioning her sexuality. She had a relationship with a woman during this time, and this relationship helped her to understand who she really was. She came out as a lesbian in 1981 and as a result of that, Billie lost all of her endorsement deals. Her marriage with Larry had ended and Billie was devastated. But this is who she was now and there was nothing she could do to change that.

Billie's life achievements

Despite her love for tennis and her struggles regarding her sexuality, Billie continued her crusade against gender inequality. She fought for the equal rights of both men and women. She received a lot of recognition for her contributions to tennis. In 1987, Billie was elected to be in the International Tennis Hall of Fame. She then became the first woman to have a major sports building named after her. The USTA National

Tennis center was renamed the USTA Billie Jean King National Tennis Centre on August 28, 2006.

In closing

In 2009, Billie Jean King was awarded the Presidential Medal of Freedom by President Barack Obama. This was the highest civilian honor awarded to Billie for her advocacy on behalf of the LGBT community. Her fight for gender equality was truly an example for the rest of the world to follow. Despite being so successful in her career, she never stopped advocating for those around her, and she always wanted fairness for all. After her divorce from her husband, she found love with Ilana Kloss, but she remains close friends with Larry and his family.

Chapter 8: The Honorable Sandra Day O'Connor

Who was Sandra Day O'Connor?

Sandra Day O'Connor is the first female associate justice of the Supreme Court in the United States. She was the first woman to be nominated for the post and the first woman who was confirmed to it. She was an attorney and a politician before she became the associate justice of the Supreme Court and she served as an associate justice from 1981 till 2006.

Sandra's background

Sandra was born on March 26th, 1930, in El Paso, Texas. Her parents were Harry Alfred Day, a rancher, and Ada Mae, a housewife. Sandra grew up on a ranch near Duncan, Arizona and the family home did not have any running water or electricity for the first seven years of Sandra's life. As a young girl, Sandra loved hunting; she owned a 22-calibre rifle and she would shoot at rabbits and coyotes. She learned to drive earlier than expected and she would change the flat tires by herself. Sandra attended a private school called Radford School for Girls, and for most of her early schooling years, she lived with her grandmother in El Paso.

Sandra graduated sixth in her class at Austin High School in 1946. She enrolled at Stanford University when she was 16 years old. She studied towards a Bachelor of Arts in Economics and she graduated with a *magna cum laude* in 1950. She then went to Stanford Law School in 1952, where she pursued her degree in Law. Sandra was given the opportunity to serve on *The Stanford Law Review* with William Rehnquist, who was the presiding editor-in-chief and later went on to become the Supreme Court chief justice. The two dated briefly in 1950 before ending their relationship when Rehnquist graduated and moved to Washington D.C.

Sandra and Jay's marriage, and career

Sandra began dating John Jay O' Conner during her last year at Stanford. John was a year behind her. The couple fell head over heels in love and within six months of her graduation, Sandra and John tied the knot at her family's ranch on the 20th of December, 1952. Sandra and John were the perfect match and they shared a special bond with each other. Despite being married so young, they both were sure of their relationship and knew what they wanted.

Sandra had some difficulty finding a job as a paid attorney because she was a woman. She then landed a job in San Mateo, California, as deputy county attorney after she agreed to work without being paid a salary and without having her own office. She had to share office space with a secretary. Sandra started earning a small salary after a few months. She wrote memos and conducted legal research during her employment. She worked with Louis Dematteis, a San Mateo district attorney and Keith Sorensen, a deputy district attorney.

Eventually, Sandra and her husband moved to Germany when he got drafted, and she worked as a civilian attorney for the Army's Quartermaster Corps. The couple lived in Germany for three years before they decided to go back to the United States to start a family. The couple welcomed three sons: Scott who was born in 1958, Brian who was born in 1960, and Jay who was born in 1962. When Brian was born, Sandra took a five-year hiatus from practising law, however, she volunteered in different political organisations and served on the presidential campaign of Arizona Senator Barry M. Goldwater in 1964.

Sandra served as an Assistant Attorney General of Arizona between 1965 and 1969. The governor of Arizona appointed Sandra to fill the vacancy in the Arizona Senate in 1969. She agreed to run for the election and she won the seat. She became the first woman to serve as a state's Majority Leader in 1973. Sandra was a star negotiator and she developed a good reputation for that. She eventually decided to leave the

Senate after serving two full terms. Sandra was then appointed to the Maricopa County Superior Court in 1974, where she served from 1975 to 1979 before she was promoted to the Arizona State Court of Appeals where she served until 1981, thereafter being appointed to the Supreme Court by President Ronald Reagan.

Her Supreme Court career

President Ronald Reagan pledged during his presidential campaign in 1980 to appoint the first woman to the Court. On July 7th, 1981, he announced that he would be nominating Sandra Day O'Connor as an Associate Justice of the Supreme Court. She would replace Potter Stewart, who was retiring. Sandra had no idea that she was being nominated until a day before the announcement was made. President Reagan had nominated Sandra on the 19th of August 1981. However, there were people who did not agree with the President's decision and they spoke out against it, such as Howard Phillips, Reverend Jerry Falwell, and Peter Gemma. They believed that Sandra was not the right person for the position as she had certain beliefs on abortion that did not sit right with certain people. Sandra's confirmation hearing was held on the 9th of September, 1981 and it was the first confirmation hearing for a Supreme Court Justice that was televised. This hearing lasted three long days and its main focus was the issues related to abortion. Sandra refused to answer any questions about her views on abortion and she did not make any impressions that she was in favor of abortion rights.

On the 21st of September, Sandra was confirmed by the U.S. Senate. She received a vote of 99-0, Senator Max Baucus was absent from the voting and he apologised to Sandra by sending her a book titled *A River Runs Through It*. She received around 60,000 public letters during her first year on the court. This was more than any other Justice in history. Sandra always felt that she had a responsibility to prove that women could successfully carry out the job of justice. Certain things had concerned her, like the lack of a lady's restroom being near the courtroom.

The New York Times decided to publish an editorial about the nine men of the Supreme Court of the Justice of the United States (SCOTUS). Sandra responded to the editor with a letter stating that the court was no longer composed of men only. There was a woman who was now a part of the Supreme Court. She referred to herself as The First Woman on the Supreme Court (FWOTSC). Sandra encouraged the Justices of the court to eat lunch together. She wanted everyone to be cordial and familiar with each other. After Sandra, Ruth Bader Ginsburg became the second female Supreme Court Justice in 1993. This brought a great amount of relief to Sandra because she was no longer the only woman on the court.

Sandra Day O'Conner oversaw many cases involving race, abortion, and foreign law. She displayed a fair and true judgement upon these cases without involving her own personal beliefs to hinder her decision-making. She was an example for women who wanted to pursue a career in law and justice. Her hard work and determination set her apart from the rest and got her noticed by many influential people. One of her great ideas while on the Supreme Court was the endorsement test, which was a way to check if the government was supporting religion.

In closing

Sandra retired from the court in 2006 and was replaced by Sam Alito. After suffering from Alzheimer's for almost 20 years, her husband passed away in 2009. On August 12, 2009, Sandra was awarded the highest civilian honor of the United States, the Presidential Medal of Freedom, which was given to her by President Barack Obama. After being diagnosed with the early stages of Alzheimer's-like dementia, Sandra retired from public life. She has a school named after her in Arizona.

Chapter 9: First Lady Michelle Obama

Who is Michelle Obama?

Michelle Obama is an American attorney and author who is married to former President of the United States, Barack Obama. She served as the first lady of the United States for eight years from 2008 till 2017. Proudly, she was the first African American woman to serve as first lady. While in office, she advocated for poverty awareness and education, and was considered a fashion icon who supported upcoming American designers. To this day, Michelle Obama is a role model to women around the world.

Michelle and her family

Born as Michelle LaVaughn Robinson, on the 17th of January 1964 in Chicago, Illinois, her parents were Fraser Robinson and Marian Shields Robinson. Her father, Fraser, worked as a water plant employee for the city, while her mother, Marian, worked as a secretary for Spiegel's catalog store, however, before that she was a full-time homemaker. Michelle's parents trace their roots back to the pre-civil war African Americans from the south. Her paternal great-grandfather, Jim Robinson, was born into slavery on Friendfield Plantation in the 1850's.

Her maternal great-grandmother, Melvinia Shields, was also born into slavery in South Carolina. She was then sold to Henry Walls Shields. She had a son who was born into slavery, and he was biracial. His father was Charles Marion Shields, brother of Henry Walls Shields. They had two more children, and after Melvina was emancipated, she lived near Shields. Michelle's family has always stated that people did not talk about slavery when they were growing up.

Michelle grew up in Chicago's South Shore community area. Her parents rented a home from their great-aunt. She describes her childhood as a conventional one. Her father would go to work every day, her mom was at home taking care of the house and every night they would have dinner around the table. Michelle loved to play the piano, as her great-aunt was a piano teacher and she taught Michelle how to play. Michelle and her family attended the South Shore United Methodist Church. Every Sunday morning the entire family would dress up and go to church together. Unfortunately, her father was sick, suffering from multiple sclerosis. This took an emotional toll on Michelle as she was growing up, and she was committed to being an excellent student at school and staying out of trouble. She didn't want to give her father any reason to stress.

Michelle's education and the beginning of her career

Michelle attended Whitney Young High School, which was Chicago's first magnet high school. This means that the school attracted learners from all over because of its specialised curricula. Michelle was on the honor roll for four years and she was a member of the National Honor Society. She was also a treasurer for the student council. In 1981, Michelle graduated as a salutatorian of her class.

Michelle went to Princeton University in 1981, where she majored in sociology. She also minored in African American studies. Michelle completed a senior thesis entitled "Princeton Educated Blacks and the Black Community." The thesis was 99 pages long and was supervised by Walter Wallace. In 1985, she graduated *cum laude* with a Bachelor of Arts. Michelle remembers how her teachers in high school had discouraged her from applying to university. They felt that she was setting her sights too high. Nonetheless, Michelle was determined and her hard work paid off.

Her time at Princeton opened her eyes to how people judged her based on her ethnicity. Her white roommate's mother tried to move her daughter to another room because Michelle was African American. These situations made Michelle more aware of her race. While studying, Michelle got involved with Carl

A. Fields Centre, a group that supported minority students. There was a daycare center which Michelle ran.

In 1988, Michelle earned herself a J.D. degree from Harvard Law School. Michelle was confident in herself and she knew what she wanted. She believed that she could be both black and brilliant. During her time at Harvard, she helped advocate for Harvard to hire professors from minority groups. She then went on to work for the Harvard Legal Aid Bureau. Michelle always believed that her education opened so many doors for her beyond even her wildest dreams.

Michelle meets Obama

Michelle and Barack Obama met at the law firm in which they were employed. The two were among the few African Americans who worked at the law firm, and she was asked to mentor Barack whilst he was a part-time associate. They began developing a relationship after a business lunch they attended, and Barack then went on to impress Michelle at a community organisation meeting. Prior to meeting Barack, Michelle was eager to focus only on her career, however, things changed as she got to know him better.

On their first date, they watched Spike Lee's movie called *Do the Right Thing* (1989). The two were so different from each other, but Barack believed that their relationship was based on an "opposites attract" situation. Michele was a stable, focused woman and Barack was more adventurous, but somehow they managed to make a great team. Michelle knew that she found the one. As they spent more time together, they fell in love and decided to get married. The couple married on October 3, 1992.

Soon after finding out that she was pregnant, Michelle suffered a miscarriage, and as a result, Michelle and Barack decided to try in vitro fertilization. The procedure was successful and the couple welcomed daughters Malia Ann, who was born in 1998, and Natasha, who was born in 2001. Michelle and Barack Obama lived on the South Side of Chicago, close to where Barack was teaching at the University of Chicago Law School. In 1996, Barack was elected to the state senate, and in 2004 he was elected as the U.S. senate. The couple decided to stay in Chicago, rather than moving to Washington D.C. because it was in the best interest of their daughters.

Michelle made a commitment to her daughters. She decided that throughout Barack's 2008 campaign for U.S. President, she would only campaign twice a week, staying away overnight only once a week to be home by the end of the second day after campaigning. She loved being a mom and she always put her children first. Michelle believed that she could still be a good mother, even whilst supporting her husband during his campaign. Michelle feared that the presidential campaign would possibly have a negative impact on her daughters. She negotiated an agreement with her husband stating that she would support him in his decision to run as president, but he had to give up smoking.

Their lives became busy and stressed. The couple barely had time to hold a conversation and they never had any time for romance. Their marriage had its ups and downs, with Barrack's political career taking off, which led to increased disagreements and arguments. He mentioned how tired and stressed the couple was during this time in his second book, *The Audacity of Hope: Thoughts on Reclaiming the American Dream.* Despite going through this tough time in their marriage, they never gave up on each other. Through scheduled date nights, they tried their best to spend as much time as possible with one another.

Michelle's daughters attended the University of Chicago Laboratory Schools. Michelle was a member of the board and she fought to maintain diversity and fairness in the University. She always believed that education was the driving force behind success and she constantly encouraged her daughters to pursue their goals and dreams. As time went on, Michelle spent more time supporting her husband's presidential campaign. In early February 2008, her participation in the campaign had increased greatly, and during this period, she attended 33 events in eight days.

Fox News described Michelle as an "Angry Black Woman," but this didn't affect her at all. Over the years, Michelle and Barack had developed a tough skin and they didn't let the opinion of others impact their lives.

They knew that there would always be criticism if they were going to constantly be in the public eye.

First Lady of the United States

Michelle embraced her duties as the First Lady of the United States. Within the first few months as First Lady, she visited soup kitchens and homeless shelters. She hosted a reception at the White House for women's rights and she advocated on behalf of military families by helping women balance their families and careers. She bonded with military families and shared in their sorrows and hardships. Michelle and Barack were awarded the Jerald Washington Memorial Founders' Award by the National Coalition for Homeless Veterans (NCHV).

She was also the only First Lady who addressed obesity and promoted good eating habits, as this was one of the leading U.S. public health crises. In 2010, she undertook her first role in the initiative to reverse the trend of childhood obesity. She believed that eating healthy, organic foods was the key to combat obesity and so she instructed the White House kitchen to buy organic foods, and she planted the first White House vegetable garden since Eleanor Roosevelt served as First Lady. In May 2014, Michelle joined a campaign to help bring back kidnapped schoolgirls from Nigeria. This was a cause which she held dear to her heart. In 2008, during the presidential campaign, Michelle and

Barack advocated for LGBTQ rights and opposed the amendments to ban same-sex marriage in the California and Florida constitutions. They supported the Illinois Gender Violence Act, the Illinois Human Rights Act, and renewed their efforts to fight against HIV and AIDS.

In closing

Michelle Obama was the first African American woman to take the place as First Lady in the United States. Throughout all of her achievements, Michelle remained humble and down to earth, and her accomplishments and impact continue today.

Chapter 10: The Girl who Fought for Education: Malala Yousafzai

Who was Malala Yousafzai?

Malala Yousafzai is a Pakistani woman who is an activist for female education, and the youngest Nobel Peace Prize winner. She is the second Pakistani to win a Nobel Prize. She is known for advocating for human rights and the education of women and children from her hometown in Khyber, Pakhtunkhwa.

Malala's background

Malala was born on July 12, 1997 in Khyber, Pakhtunkhwa province in Pakistan. She was born at home because the family couldn't afford a hospital. She was born into a lower-middle-class family that is Sunni Muslim. Her family's ethnicity was Pashtun and they belonged to the Yusufzai tribe. Her parents are

Ziauddin Yousafzai and Tor Pekai Yousafzai. Her name, Malala, means "grief-stricken" and she was named after a famous Pashtun poet, Malalai of Maiwand, who was a warrior woman from southern Afghanistan.

Malala lived with her parents and her two younger brothers who were named Atal and Khushal. She is fluent in speaking Urdu, Pashto, and English. Her father educated her, he was a poet, and he owned a few private schools named the Khushal Public School. Ziauddin was also an activist for education. Malala had always wanted to become a doctor, however, her father encouraged her to become a politician. He knew that his daughter was special and he would stay up with her at night and talk about politics.

Malala was inspired by Prime Minister Benazir Bhutto and Muhammad Ali Jinnah, the founder of Pakistan. She began speaking on education rights in September of 2008 when she was 11-12 years old. Her father wanted her to speak at a local press club in Peshawar. Her speech was covered by television stations and newspapers, and in her speech, Malala asked how the Taliban could take away her basic right to education. In 2009, she worked as a trainee at the Institute for War and Peace Reporting's Open Minds Pakistan Youth programme and was later promoted to peer educator. Malala helped learners engage in discussions that were constructive on social issues. She did this through public debates, dialogues, and journalism.

The dangerous but courageous act

Aamer Ahmed Khan, who worked for the BBC Urdu website, came up with a new way of covering the Taliban's growing influence in Swat. They asked a schoolgirl to blog about her life in Swat anonymously. They had been in touch with Ziauddin, Malala's father, but he could not find any students who were willing to take on this task because their families felt it was too dangerous. So, Ziauddin suggested that Malala, who was 11 years old at the time, take on the task and report about the Taliban anonymously. During that time, a man named Maulana Fazlullah, was leading the Tehrik-i-Taliban Pakistan militants, who were quickly taking over Swat.

The Taliban banned music, television, and education for girls and women going shopping. Their heinous acts were evident for all to see as bodies of beheaded policemen were being displayed around town. There was a girl named Aisha who went to Malala's father's school. She wanted to write a diary, but her parents didn't allow her to because they were afraid of the Taliban. Their only alternative was Malala, who was in seventh grade at that time. The people at the BBC wanted to protect Malala's identity so they told her to use another name in her blogs. The blogs were published under the name "Gul Makai," which means cornflower.

How Malala's activism began

Malala's blog ended on March 12, 2009, and she was interviewed by numerous TV stations and her identity as the girl who wrote those blogs about the Taliban was revealed in December of 2009. She also used these TV appearances as an opportunity to advocate for female education. She was the chair of the District Child Assembly of the Khpal Foundation from 2009 till 2010. Malala trained with a girls' empowerment organisation in 2011. The organisation was run by Gulalai Ismail and was called Aware Girls. He taught them how to fight for girls' rights to an education peacefully, without resorting to violence.

A South African activist, Archbishop Desmond Tutu, nominated Malala for the International Children's Peace Prize in October, 2011. She was the first Pakistani girl who had been nominated for this great award. However, the award was won by Michaela Mycroft from South Africa. On December 19, 2011, Malala was awarded the National Peace Award for Youth by Prime Minister Yousaf Raza Gillani. The prime minister directed that an IT campus be set up in the Swat Degree College for Women as Malala had requested. A secondary school was also named after her.

As she became more recognised around the world, the more dangerous it became for Malala. There were death threats that were published in newspapers, and these newspapers were slipped under her door. She also began receiving threats on her social media accounts. The spokesperson for the Taliban said that they were forced to act and in a meeting which was held in 2012, they agreed to kill her. Malala was shot by a Taliban gunman on the 9th of October in 2012, as she was travelling home on a bus. She was just 15 years old at the time. There were two other girls who had been wounded as well in that attack, Kainat Riaz and Shazia Ramzan.

Damaged by the bullet, Malala sustained injuries to the left side of her brain. A portion of her skull had to be removed, a decompressive craniectomy, to allow room for the swelling in her brain. She was treated by numerous doctors in Germany and England, and on October 17, she woke up from her coma. She recovered and was released from the hospital on the 3rd of January in 2013, however, she had to undergo further surgeries in the future. There were protests that took place against the shooting and over two million people signed a petition for the Right to Education campaign.

Madonna, an American singer, dedicated a song to Malala called "Human Nature" at a concert in Los Angeles the day of the attack. Angelina Jolie donated $200,000 to the Malala Fund for Girls Education. The United Nations launched a petition in Malala's name. They supported what Malala fought for and the demand of the petition was that no child should be left out of school by the year 2015. They called to Pakistan to plan and deliver education for every child, they called for all countries to stop the discrimination against girls, and they wanted the international organisations to make sure that the 61 million children who were out of school, would be back in school by the end of 2015.

In closing

Malala Yousafzai is a remarkable woman who advocated for the right to education for girls in Pakistan. She didn't let fear get the best of her; instead, she stood firm in her fight for education. Despite being a victim of attempted murder by the Taliban, she never lost hope or retracted in fear.

Honorable Mentions

Traditionally, women have been considered defenseless, weak, timid, and powerless human beings. They have consistently been looked down upon, robbed of their rights and silenced by men, be it their husbands, their fathers, or their brothers. However, the women in this book have found ways to rise above it all. They have taken a stand for what they believe in and they have advocated for those who could not stand up for themselves. These women have changed the world in their own way, from being the first woman to fly solo across the Atlantic Ocean to becoming the first African American First Lady of the United States.

Women like: Kalpana Chawla, the first Indian woman to fly in space; Donyale Luna, the first black supermodel; Florence Griffith Joyner, the world's fastest woman; and Raye Montague, who developed a computer program that changed the way Navy ships were designed. Each and every accomplishment these women achieved didn't come for free and was not easy. They worked hard and didn't give up on themselves or on those whom they were fighting for.

Conclusion

The willingness and determination of these women is an inspiration to us all, and it motivates us to fight for our rights and for the rights of others. Women have something special inside of them which sets them apart from men: Their passion, drive, and willpower is amazing. They have proved to us that no matter what anyone says, it is possible to achieve your dreams and make a difference in the world. Even the smallest act of kindness can turn into something remarkable. Their legacy will live on long after they've gone.

References

Amelia Earhart - The Official Licensing Website of Amelia Earhart. (2015). Amelia Earhart. https://ameliaearhart.com

Cook., E.T. (1913). *The Life of Florence Nightingale.* Vol 1, pg 237.

First Lady Michelle Obama. (2016, February 11). Whitehouse.gov; Whitehouse. https://obamawhitehouse.archives.gov/administration/first-lady-michelle-obama

Florence Nightingale. (2021, September 24). Wikipedia. https://en.wikipedia.org/wiki/Florence_Nightingale#Crimean_War

History.com Editors. (2009, November 9). *Rosa Parks.* HISTORY; A&E Television Networks. https://www.history.com/topics/black-history/rosa-parks

International Tennis Hall of Fame. (2019). Tennisfame.com. https://www.tennisfame.com/hall-of-famers/inductees/billie-jean-king

Kettler, S. (2018, March 29). *Malala Yousafzai*. Biography. https://www.biography.com/activist/malala-yousafzai

Marie Curie. (2019). Marie Curie. https://www.mariecurie.org.uk

Smentkowski, B. P. (2019). Sandra Day O'Connor | Biography & Facts. In *Encyclopædia Britannica*. https://www.britannica.com/biography/Sandra-Day-OConnor

The Editors of Encyclopedia Britannica. (2019a). Emmeline Pankhurst | Biography & Facts. In *Encyclopædia Britannica*. https://www.britannica.com/biography/Emmeline-Pankhurst

The Editors of Encyclopedia Britannica. (2019b). Emmeline Pankhurst | Biography & Facts. In *Encyclopædia*

Britannica.

https://www.britannica.com/biography/Emmeline-Pankhurst

The Editors of Encyclopedia Britannica. (2019c). Coretta Scott King | Biography & Facts. In *Encyclopædia Britannica.*

https://www.britannica.com/biography/Coretta-Scott-King

Printed in Great Britain
by Amazon